Doctor
RANKIN
of Carluke

JAMES ELDER

CORRYVRECKAN

Published in Great Britain by Corryvreckan Books
www.corryvreckanbooks.co.uk

Copyright © James Elder, 2023

British Library Cataloguing-in-Publication Data
A catalogue record for this book is available on
request from the British Library.

ISBN: 978-1-7384019-0-1

Cover image: *Doctor Rankin of Carluke*
Photographic portrait by James Valentine, Dundee.
Courtesy of Dr Peter J. Gordon.

NOTE

THE STORIES narrated herein [as part of a fictional retelling by Dr Rankin of his own life story – JE] have come from many sources.

It is impossible now to vouch for their truth in every detail. The stories have been told so often, and by so many tongues, that they may have acquired some of the characteristics of traditional folklore.

In the course of their passage through two generations some of them could hardly have escaped the influence of that popular imagination and creative instinct which have moulded the world's greatest epics.

But many of these stories of the "Rankin Cycle" are still told by people from first hand recollections, and I am convinced that they are substantially true, and that they are characteristic both of the man and of the place.

ALEXANDER MACCALLUM SCOTT M.P.
JUNE 1916

CARLUKE and The Fruit Lands

KEY PLACES IN THE TEXT

Overtown

Worsley hill

Garrion Burn

Jellyfield

Garrion Burn

Brownlee Ho.

Cairdie's brig

Dalserf Holm Kirk

Mauldslie Castle

Mauldslie Road

Whiteshaw

Schools

Our House

Cadger's Dub

Manse Church

To Carnwath

CARLUKE

Kirkton Ho.

Jock's Burn

TO GLASGOW

Milton Road

Milton Ho.

Wellens

CARLUKE

Buttelhead Road

Lanark Road

DALSERF

The Holm

Stewart Hall

Poplarhill

Braidwood Ho.

Gowanglen

Braidwood

Midtoun

The Yett

The Heids

Swinstie Hill

Orchard Ho.

Ha'-bar

Coalshott

The Dales

Brownlie

Fiddler Burn

Crossford

Mashock Burn

Lee Ho.

Creignethan Castle (ruins)

River Nethan

Clyde

LANARK

LESMAHAGOW

To LANARK

Stonebyres Ho.

For a larger map visit www.corryvreckanbooks.co.uk

Contents

The "Auld Lichts"

E VERY TIME you pass Market Place in Carluke, I would urge you to imagine this scene:

At the corner of Market Place and North Lane* stood a one-storey house with a sturdy roof of thatched straw and a storm-battered wooden door.

That was my family home. However, do not let your mind's-eye be fooled by its humble appearance. In future years the visitors knocking on my door came from all corners of the country, among them the most celebrated scientists, writers, and artists of the day.

It was in this house, on Tuesday, 26th of March 1805, that I, Daniel Reid Rankin, was born. The ninth child and fifth son of James and Isobel Rankin. They were ordinary, working class folk.

My father was a souter,† an important skill in a village populated for the most part by families of cottage weavers. He was a devoutly religious Auld Licht‡ who demanded piety to God and strict obedience to Scripture.

My mother was the daughter of John Reid, the farmer of Bankbrae. She was a naturally lively person, whose spirits were a little subdued by the prevailing atmosphere of sternness in our household.

---

* *North Lane* later re-named Rankin Street
† *souter* shoemaker
‡ *Auld Licht* Old Light

Near our house were my father's workshops, where he spent his life making and mending people's boots and shoes. And when he wasn't fixing shoes, he was at the church – praying for Salvation.

All of us were Sinners, but God had chosen a limited number of souls to which He had unconditionally granted Salvation – the so-called "Elect".

God alone knew who was "of the Elect" and who wasn't, and so those who hoped to go to Heaven prayed a lot and kept their fingers crossed.

The Auld Lichts believed in the real, lurid existence of Hell, and that rigid rules of behaviour had been set out in the Bible, which the Civil Magistrate had a duty to impose on the people.

If you misbehaved, you'd wind up on the "cutty-stool"* – a black-painted platform in front of the pulpit – to be told off in front of your family and friends and later frowned upon by the whole village.

One Sabbath evening, when I was five, my father asked me if I loved God.

'No!' I replied stoutly.

The family held their breath in horror, waiting for his anger to break.

'Why not?' he asked.

'Because he burns folk,' I said solemnly.

No sound could be heard except the ticking of the clock. Then, without a word, the poor man stood up and went out to the back garden, where he spent a long time mulling over my answer. He never referred to the matter again.

---

* "*cutty-stool*" the stool of repentance

I staunchly refused to go to church, which, in those days, was too incredible for most to contemplate, never mind accept.

I loathed pretentiousness, ostentation and cant, and made no secret of my impatience with the narrower forms of religion. My comments to a farmer called Sandy Paterson were the talk of the town. Whenever I saw him heading for church I would call: 'Going for your Sunday's sleep, Sandy?' At which he would laugh to himself and mutter: 'Queer chiel,* queer chiel!'

But behind closed doors the stricter Auld Lichts were not amused. They called me "hellish Dan", and my unorthodox views were to cost me dear – in a way I could never have foreseen.

---

* *chiel* young man

9

KAY'S SCHOOL

I ATTENDED the parish school, which stood at The Cross at the head of the High Street, where the National Bank now stands.

The Schoolmaster was a man called James Kay, a native of Walston near Carnwath. Mr Kay was a scholar, and a well informed man; but, perhaps, about one of the worst teachers. He was, however, when in the mood, among the best anecdotists, of local range, that lived in his time. Some of his stories, of a personal kind, are racy, and well worth repeating.

He had undertaken to get and bring from Lanark an umbrella, which an ingenious smith had promised to mend for a lady in the neighbourhood. On his return home the day happened to be wet, and he used the umbrella to protect himself.

On reaching the village, before gaining his own house, he had to traverse the entire street within direct observation of the windows of his house – had passed the Cross well, and was scarcely twenty paces from the front door – when, suddenly, it opened, and his old mother stood in the way, as if to hinder farther progress, uttering in a loud voice of lamentation: 'O, Jamie Kay – Jamie Kay – wae's* me to live to see you

---

* wae's woe is

ack sic a pairt in this vain flirdmagarie world:* wow –
wow, Jamie Kay! hoo daur ye stan' afore the Almichty,†
wi' that emblem o' Satan o'er ye'er head,‡ to kepp aff
His blissings that fa' baith§ on the just and unjust!'

This scene took place about ten years before the
close of the past century, and proves that even the
umbrella (then a considerable time in use in some
places), had not been introduced without the usual
protest on religious grounds. Janet Kay was an old
woman of strong opinions, and strong will, which her
heir and representative had learned never to question,
for the sake of peace and decorum; nor did he at this
time defend himself, but peacefully aimed to get
towards the door.

'Na-na, – na-na, it canna be here, it winna ‖ be here,
the byre's guid enough for't.'¶ So the lady's umbrella
was housed for the night with the cow; and Janet's son
silently sought comfort and consolation from under the
lid of his snuff-box, dreading that words might be
dangerous with the umbrella so near.

Mr Kay had a sprinkling of irony and fun in his
vitals, which would break out at times. The modern
style of Latin pronunciation gave him rare amusement.
He would repeat lines of favourite authors, in the soft
accent – (English manner) – with an air of contempt,

---

* *ack sic a pairt in this vain flirdmagarie world* act such a part in
this vain peacocky world
† *hoo daur ye stan' afore the Almichty* how dare you stand before
the Almighty
‡ *emblem o' Satan o'er ye'er head* emblem of Satan over your head
§ *to kepp aff His blissings that fa' baith* to ward off His blessings
that fall both
‖ *na-na, it canna, it winna* no, no, it cannot, it will not
¶ *byre's guid enough for't* cowshed's good enough for it

and in curious mawkish tones, at which he laughed and coughed, and coughed and laughed, so outrageously, that all watching him did the same, more, of course, from the apparently insane efforts of the mimic than at the intrinsic cause. It was droll* to see Mr Kay droll! He would stretch out his hand, and screw up his mouth, uttering, in the manner stated:

'Tityre tu, patulae recumbans sub tegmine fagi'–[†]

a line from Virgil suiting his purpose, ending with the exclamation: 'Did ever mortal man listen to gibberish like that!'

Like the other village schoolboys, I wore a moleskin jacket, corduroy trousers, and the Scottish blue bonnet. The books we had were the Wee Spell, the Big Spell, the Shorter Catechism,[‡] and the Bible. I was particularly good at the catechism so, in my earlier years, I never got a thrashing. But, during my rebellious youth, I baited Mr Kay along with all the other boys. He called us "a parcel of wild boars from the mountains".

On one occasion he punished me, and in revenge I lifted one of the peats stacked beside the fire and hurled it at him, knocking him off his stool. From that moment on, I was known as "Danny, the devil".

---

* *droll* slightly crazed
[†] 'You, Tityrus, 'neath a broad beech-canopy/ Reclining –'
[‡] *Catechism* questions and answers about religious beliefs

AN OBJECT OF INTEREST

N O MORE THAN OUTSIDE A DOOR, from which issued a mingling of smells all but tangible, comprehending tansy, burgundy-pitch, ham-and-eggs in particular, unnameable compounds in general, the passage within being hung with numerous bundles of what seemed to be withered nettles, horse gowans, docken* roots and so forth, called herbs, there stood a figure familiar to all in Carluke parish, one who was something above or below the common – an object of interest.

Broad shoulders – large body – short arms – shorter legs – a considerable head, mostly face, set on shoulders, with the neck a-wanting. That face, red, fleshy and unsmooth, was furnished with a mouth ample and, it may be, suitable; a nose warty and rosy which all but wagged on gravitation principles; ears laid on a cushion of puffy buff-leather-looking material, making an unseemly claim to be part of that already big bare red face; a brow overlaid, as if for protection, by strong whitish hairs smooth as comb could make them; eyes, firm, restless, well-set, and bespeaking intelligence, which added greatly to humanize, nay ornament, a face that needed some such modifying power; and behind all, a strong head of hair, white with a decided tinge of unpleasant yellow, combed so much forward, so much downwards towards the ears, so much backward, which

---

* *docken* dock plant

13

last disposition of the hair necessarily overhung the coat neck. What a study! The dress no artist ever shaped or could shape if he tried, and no tailor ever served the coat that would fit, in the strict artistic meaning of the word, that figure; yet the article worn fitted well enough, one might say, by covering the whole man, if the outrageous bulgings, wrinklings, and that ungraceful hang of garment go unnoticed. There might be and very likely there was a vest, which the ample coat concealed, and there might be a shirt, collar and tie, lost to view; but breeches there was surely, for at the knees, which were uncommonly near the ground, certain dingy strings, by which that article of dress was usually fastened, dangled over a limited surface of hairy skin made too evident to the spectator by the slight falling down of a blue stocking, which in wrinkled fashion covered as shapeless a leg as could well be – the feet being pretty deeply into shoes, ample and good, with large buckles in front, bent down at the heel to serve the present but temporary use of slippers . . .

This was Doctor Weir, the doctor of the village, who had been practising as usual, fair weather or foul, his airing before breakfast. A rare character in more senses than one, he was never an unwelcome visitor at the school – not on account of his talents, or virtues, or good manners; but more likely that he lacked everything such – possessing, however, a rambling share of common sense in matters within his comprehension – censorious not a little, and garrulous and amusing without intention – the Navy, where he had served in the cock-pit, being the stock from which he drew.

One afternoon, the doctor, without the ceremony of a knock, shuffled, as usual, into the school, and up to the desk, at *his* full speed, producing a scrap of paper with an air of excessive bluntness, answering for dignity. Mr Kay quickly scanned the document without betraying a particle of surprise. He laid it aside, saying – pleasantly for him – 'I'm going to dismiss the school presently.'

'What's that to me?' said the other, 'sign the line.'

Still, the schoolmaster tendered some gentle evasion.

'Come, come,' blustered the medical man, in his blustering way, 'I've no time to waste – put down your name, that's all – put down your name.'

'Wait one minute,' said Mr Kay, uneasiness beginning to work the features of the irritable, but on this occasion, patient schoolmaster, 'and I'll write a certificate in place of this.'

'No, no – d— me! what's that? I've no time to wait, I tell you, no time to wait.'

'Well,' replied Mr Kay, his tongue curiously at work beneath his under lip, and his eyes kindled by a strange light, evidently on the verge of an outbreak – 'I cannot put my name to that document.'

This was a certificate for exemption from the militia, requiring a doctor, and minister or elder's affirmation, of which Kay was the latter.

'No! What for no?' roared the doctor in an irritating key. Mr Kay, roused to the point where bitterness ran over, said, very crushingly: 'What for, Sir? To be plain with you, it's neither written nor spelled!'

'Ba–ba! Whew!!' uttered the medical practitioner, adding defiantly, tauntingly, and loudly: 'Whae the deval[*] cares for spelling noo-a-days?'[†]

---

[*] *whae the deval* who the devil
[†] *noo-a-days* nowadays

Robert Hunter, M.D.

At sixteen, I was apprenticed as a writer* to Vary & Hewitt, a firm of solicitors in Lanark. By eighteen, I was studying law at Glasgow University. And that's where I met Robert Hunter, M.D.

Courtesy of University of Glasgow Archives & Special Collections

Of course, he wasn't quite "M.D." yet, but he had been studying medicine for six years, and planned to graduate in another two. He was ten years older than I,

---
* *writer* lawyer

wore the scarlet gown and black silk top hat of the matriculated student, and was already lecturing on anatomy at Portland Street Medical School.

We met at the Hamilton Building of the College in High Street, which housed both the Law and Anatomy Class-rooms. His tales of surgical dissections were vastly more interesting than the dull law lectures I attended. I began to borrow his books and join him in some of the medical classes. At last I had stumbled on the career I had been looking for.

At the time, I was depute clerk to William Vary at the Justice of the Peace Clerk's Office in Wilson Street. I applied to the university authorities to switch from law to medicine and, to my delight, was given consent.

Soon after, I abandoned my post in the law office. Mr Vary was understandably dismayed at losing his depute clerk, but I think he admired my pluck.

I began studying medicine, financing myself from my meagre savings. For the next few years I took classes in anatomy, surgery and medical practice, and even learned how to relieve nerve pain in teeth! I was often disheartened at the enormity of the task I had set myself, and more often I was hungry and cold, but never once did I consider giving up.

Students did a lot of heavy drinking, which I loathed. At one dinner party the ladies retired and the doors were locked to ensure privacy. A disgusting debauch followed with young men huddled in helpless confusion under the dinner table. I left the house rather than participate.

Finally, I had found my true vocation – and I intended to succeed!

THE FAMOUS SAW-BONE CUTTER

M Y FAVOURITE UNIVERSITY PROFESSOR was Dr James Jeffray, who held the strange double Chair of Anatomy and Botany. His daughter, Miss Jeffray, owned Milton estate near Carluke.

In 1827 Professor Jeffray was still a strong, tall, venerable man of 68 with a head of white hair, well comporting with the white robes he then wore, resembling as nearly as possible a bishop's gown with lawn* sleeves.

He had more than two hundred students, many of them Army and Navy surgeons learning how to amputate limbs during battle. In the 1780s he claimed to have conceived the idea of the surgical chain saw, used to remove damaged sections of bone in an accurate manner.

Dr Jeffray lived in House No. 1 of Professors' Court, one of twelve official residences in a large courtyard adjoining the College. The west end of his house stood back a few feet from the line of High Street, and between it and the mass of wretched dwellings that composed the Havanna, a small outhouse intervened, to be used along with it. This the Professor did not require and, towards the end of 1821, being of a penurious† disposition, he converted the building into a shop and let

---

* *lawn* fine linen
† *penurious* money-grubbing

18

it to Peter Cook, a dealer of hams and cheeses, without first obtaining the consent of the College Faculty.

Many letters appeared in the newspapers complaining of this non-academic use of a University building. In a facetious letter in the Glasgow Chronicle, 11 December 1821, one citizen wrote:

> Mr. Simon Syntax, my neighbour, . . . speaks of a shop within the precincts of the College as a disgrace to literature. He talks highly of the indignation which such a prostitution would excite in the minds of Hutcheson, Smith and Reid.[*] He boasts of a Teacher of his own, one whom he familiarly calls *Jolly Jack Phosphorus*,[†] who according to his account was in his day a great enemy to lucre-loving professors. Mr. Syntax often swears (for warm indignation will make any one swear) that had this philosopher been alive at the present time he would have planted his far-famed cannon on the opposite side of the street and would have plied hard against the obnoxious shop till he had laid its stone and timbers together with its hams, its cheeses and its butter all in one undistinguished mass of ruin.

With public outrage threatening to erupt, the Faculty wrote to Jeffray objecting to the shop, and although the Professor promised to restore it to its former purpose, he made no haste to do so.

---

[*] *Hutcheson, Smith and Reid* former Chairs of Moral Philosophy at Glasgow University

[†] *Jolly Jack Phosphorus* John Anderson, a Jacobite soldier who designed a cannon during the 1740s uprising, and submitted it to the French Revolutionary Government; also a former Professor of Natural Philosophy at Glasgow University

A certain fiddle-playing wag affixed the following squib[*] to the door:

This once was Dr Jeffray's shop,
The famous saw-bone cutter,
But now it's let to Peter Cook
For selling bread and butter!
– *Blind Alick*

On 20th December 1821, the Faculty peremptorily[†] ordered that the shop should be shut by 3rd January, and appointed a Committee to see their order carried out and, if needful, to take steps along with the College Law Agent to have the tenant summarily removed.

At length, the shop was shut.

---

[*] *squib* a short, humorous piece
[†] *peremptorily* unconditionally

MARION

IN SUMMER, medical lectures began in May and ended in July, which left three months free until the start of the winter session. During this time I returned home and lived with my parents. It was in one of these long breaks that a family of distant relations came from Edinburgh to spend summer with us in Carluke.

Marion was only 12 when I first met her, and at first I simply regarded her as "my little cousin". She was a very intelligent child, who shared my delight in nature and art.

Full of grace and gaiety, she gazed intently as I pointed out the flowers, birds and rocks on our long walks in the country. We became great friends, and people declared I was spoiling her.

Later on, I got a pony for Marion, and we scampered happily over the countryside on horseback, visiting the Falls of Clyde, Craignethan Castle, and Hamilton Palace.

Willans, a smallholding on the Milton estate, was a favourite calling place, where we could talk to John Greenshields, the sculptor, and watch him at work. He undertook to make a portrait of Marion when she was older.

As the years passed, Marion grew into a beautiful young woman and my kindliness towards her grew into love. She returned my feelings.

We were both fond of music. I was a good singer, and played the flute. I gave her lessons in singing. Her companionship became a joy to me.

When she returned to town I wrote her every week, sending a flower, a book, something to delight her. One of my gifts was a little herbarium in which these verses were written:

FORGET–ME–NOT

I've gathered thee these flowerets fair
   From many a hill and many a dell,
And placed them with some little care
   To suit my taste and please thee well.
But of the flowers that deck my gift,
   Whate'er their beauty, one I've got,–
One sweeter far to me than all,
   Though simple; 'tis Forget-me-not.

If far removed by death or change,
   And memory may no longer bear
The semblance of the giver's face,–
   The face of him who *would* be dear;
This little pledge of friendship may,
   Although mislaid or long forgot,
Again come to your gentle hands
   And aid my prayer, "Forget me not."

Time passed, and nothing occurred to mar our perfect friendship. I continued to send her gifts, book after book; one taking the form of an album of my own poems.

The last of these was written just before her final visit to Carluke, when she was sixteen years old. It was called "ANTICIPATION", and these are some of its verses:

O is she still, or not the same
　　As at the last farewell?
Or is she changed? At any change
　　My feelings must rebel.

I could not live my mind at ease
　　If chang-ed be her heart;
No balm could heal so quick a wound
　　I could not live – and part.

She is – I know she is – the same
　　No change will mark her brow;
Each feature brightened with delight
　　To-morrow's sun will show.

It was understood I would propose to Marion when she was eighteen. There was every reason to believe her reply would be favourable. Both sets of parents were delighted.

A Licence to Practise

For a time during my college career I was assistant to Robert Hunter, M.D. Yes, that's right! He had finally graduated as a doctor of medicine aged 33, and not long after, was appointed Professor of Anatomy at the newly opened Anderson's University building in George Street.

On one occasion Professor Hunter was absent and I was asked to lecture in his place. This prospect so alarmed me it brought on a haemorrhage, and I collapsed in the street. Passers-by identified me from a letter found in my pocket, and had me taken to my lodgings.

In 1829, after completing my own medical studies, I obtained my licence to practise from the Royal College of Physicians and Surgeons of Glasgow.

I was thrilled to be offered a promising post as assistant professor, although at some distance from my parents' home in Carluke. I accepted gladly, with visions of future glory swimming before my eyes.

But, on the evening before I was due to depart, I discovered my mother weeping bitterly as she packed my trunk.

'What is the matter, mother?' I asked anxiously.

'O laddie!' she sobbed, wiping away a tear, 'it will break my heart to part with you.'

I immediately sent a letter resigning the appointment. Shortly afterwards, I resolved to open a doctor's practice in Carluke, where, in spite of protestations from my more scholarly friends, I remained ever after.

DOCTOR DAN

IN 1830 the village of Carluke was a small one, and its only industry a dying one. The stagnation that followed the Napoleonic Wars had hit the cottage weavers severely and the mining revolution that followed had administered the final blow.

The wider parish of Carluke, then as now, consisted of the mansions and orchards in the valley of the Clyde, and a belt of agricultural land stretching between the river and the high moorlands. In this district, then, partly industrial and partly rural, I settled down to my work among the people.

To help me cover the miles of my broad practice, I was gifted an infamous jet-black horse that no one else could manage. Mostly, he just neighed and snorted, but sometimes he'd rear up on his hind legs and lash out with his hoofs. On two occasions he threw me.

Fortunately, I was a grand rider, and people eventually got used to seeing me hurtling across the fields, hanging on for dear life as I rushed to some medical emergency.

My mode of dress was that of the professional man of my youth. Imagine a tall-looking gent, dressed in tight-fitting surtout coat with flowing frock, tight knee breeches, high Hessian boots, and a tall silk hat. I was very particular concerning my appearance, and always kept my clothes neat and spotless.

My hair was reddish yellow, and flowed in straight lines to my shoulders. In my early days it stuck out in a sort of wave over my collar and, after removing my hat, I had a habit of intensifying this by running my fingers through my "mane". On wet days it was always tied at the end and tucked away under my hat.

My brow is high and broad, the eyebrows bushy and fair, the blue eyes big and, some say, expressive.

DOCTOR DAN
Courtesy of Dr Peter J. Gordon

The artist who took this photograph begged of me a front view. I refused the request by informing him I could see my face at any time by looking in the glass. What I wished was a view of my back.

I tried to maintain on my clean-shaved face a picture of benevolent calm, as properly befits a doctor. I carried myself with great dignity, which made me seem to some as if I was an inhabitant of the previous century, instead of the one in which I lived.

To children I had a curious, fanciful way of speaking, which appealed to their imaginations. Promising the gift of a knife to one little boy, I said: 'I've a fine gold lancet* lying at hame† among some auld horse-shoon.'‡

A small girl saw an anatomical specimen in my house and asked to have it. 'We'll see,' I said. 'Bring a great lapful of cabbages on Sunday to feed it.' I warned young Agnes, my servant, to receive the cabbages with due solemnity when they came. It is wrong to disappoint a child.

During my life the wheel of fashion twice came round full circle, but I never altered my style of dress, my long hair, or my old-fashioned ways.

---

* *lancet* a surgical knife
† *hame* home
‡ *horse-shoon* horseshoes

HOUSE CALLS

A S A DOCTOR, I had the entrée to every house in the parish – from castle to cot. I never knocked, but walked right in like a member of the family. Sometimes I would arrive on a house call by jumping my horse clear over the wall into the garden – and leave in the same way.

When Willie Forrest of The Yett was an infant his mother took him up to Carluke to visit her husband's people. Shortly after she arrived she was sitting before the fire washing the child when I entered the room unannounced. Without uttering a word I lifted the boy from her lap by his foot and held him out at arm's length. She had never seen me before but had heard much about me, and guessing who I was, sat still without showing any signs of alarm. I replaced the child on her lap and told her: 'Ay* lassie, ye have a guid nerve!'

A patient suffering from a very bad quinsy,† or, as we called it, "a beeling‡ throat", was sitting wrapped up at the fireside. I pulled my chair up to the fire and talked to her in a very sympathetic way.

---

* *Ay* Yes
† *quinsy* inflammation of the tonsils
‡ "*beeling*" festering

Taking up the poker, I commenced to "ripe up"[*] the fire, and absent-mindedly left it sticking between the ribs. Suddenly, I pulled it out red-hot and made a lunge as if I were going to thrust it at her feet. She jumped up with a scream, and, as I had anticipated, the sudden jerk broke the abscess and gave her relief.

At one woman's house I found no one at home, so I took all the chairs in the sitting room and arranged them in the middle of the floor. Next time I met her, I said: 'I called the other day, but there was no one at home, so I just left my card.' 'Ay,' she replied, 'I saw it when I got home.'

In another case my patient was convalescent after a long illness. I complimented her on her pluck and endurance.

She said: 'Now that I'm getting better, Doctor, what will be the best thing for me to eat?'

I replied: 'You might try a dish of horse-shoe nails fried in butter!' I regarded her recovery as complete.

A fond mother was much concerned about the health of her son. The father was a baker, and the root of the trouble, as I suspected, was that the boy got too much pastry to eat out of the shop.

After studying the case I pronounced it a serious one, which would require a drastic course of poulticing.

'An oatmeal poultice is the thing,' I said. 'Apply one night and morning for a month. I think that'll shift the trouble.'

'Is it as bad as that?' exclaimed the anxious mother, adding: 'And how do you make an oatmeal poultice?'

---

[*] "*ripe up*" clear of ash

'Just as if ye were makin' parritch* – the very same.'
'And where is the poultice to be applied?'
'Internally! Internally! Jist let him eat it!'

---

* *makin' parritch* making porridge

Meanness

M Y GENERAL CUSTOM was to treat the poor without fee. When asked for a bill I'd say: 'I'll tell you when I need the money,' or, when returning a cheque tendered in payment for medical attendance, I'd add this note:

> I despair of finding the time for account making up. As a relief to us both, you can hand me the amount next time you see me.

My paying patients were mostly the gentry of the parish. One wealthy lady asked me to treat her trivial ailments, day and night, for months. I sent her a brief account; a sum rounded down to my cost:

To Medical Attendance £10

She returned the bill, and insisted she would pay nothing until she had seen a complete list all of her treatments. I wrote out the long list and sent it back with a bill for double the amount. She paid the bill, but I never attended on her again.

One man, who called to pay his account, lingered unnecessarily. I told him: 'You owed me nothing when you came in. Now you owe me three shillings.'

A widow of my acquaintance was in dire straits because her miserly son had failed to hand over the allowance to which she was entitled. I sent the son a medical bill for £80. He expressed his astonishment at the figure, but I assured him there was a record of every visit. Ultimately the amount was paid, and with the notes in my hand I walked straight to the old lady's house and handed her the money.

Jamie Prentice, better known as "Brew", had the reputation of being terribly near.[*] One day, I overtook him struggling up the road to his house wheeling a barrow full of coals.

'Hullo Brew,' I exclaimed. 'What are you pechin' an' makin' sic a fuss aboot?'[†]

'Deed Doctor, this is nae licht wecht.[‡] I'd gladly gie ye a shillin' to tak'[§] the barrow-load up to my door.'

'Done wi' ye!' I said, and seizing the handles of the barrow, I wheeled it right up to his door.

'Faith Doctor! I didna' think ye could hae[‖] done it,' said Brew.

'O, that's naething,[¶] but what aboot the shillin'?'

'O Doctor, I never meant that. It was just my joke!'

'It was nae joke wi' me, an' I want that shillin'.'

'But ye kent[**] I was jist in fun.'

'No fun about it. I must have the shillin' ye promised me.'

---

[*] *near* miserly
[†] *pechin' an' makin' sic a fuss aboot* gasping and making such a fuss about
[‡] *nae licht wecht* no light weight
[§] *tak'* take
[‖] *hae have*
[¶] *naething* nothing
[**] *kent knew*

'But Doctor – I havena'* got a shillin'.'

'Then awa'† in to the wife an' get it.'

Brew trudged reluctantly into the house and brought back a shilling between his finger and thumb. Holding it out half-heartedly, he protested: 'It was just in fun Doctor, but there it is. Though I ken‡ ye'll no take it.'

I took it without compunction.

'Hey, Rob,' I cried to a neighbour working in his garden next door, 'put that in the plate next Sabbath,' and tossed the shilling over the hedge to him.

---

* *havena'* haven't
† *awa'* away
‡ *ken* know

ENVIOUS TONGUES

SUMMER ARRIVED and, with it, a note from Marion. It said, perhaps she might not get to Carluke. I replied, telling her I would come to Edinburgh myself and bring her back with me.

When I called at her parents' house, she and her mother were entertaining guests. On hearing my voice, Marion anxiously rushed to meet me, but her mother interposed and came to the door alone. Abruptly, and unexpectedly, I found my suit rejected.

The shock cut me to the heart. A haemorrhage started and blood rushed from my mouth. Marion was with difficulty prevented from participating in this painful scene. The doors were shut, and eventually I recovered sufficiently to go away.

Why had her mother rejected me? I had a thriving medical practice, there was no other suitor, and I was sure Marion loved me. There was only one possible reason: the wagging of envious tongues!

Tittle-tattle about my unorthodox views on religion had reached the ears of Marion's mother. She had hardened her heart against me and decided I was not the man for her daughter.

She never altered her opinion, and I never stopped loving Marion.

Some years later, Marion married. I maintained an interest in her welfare from afar, and showed much unobtrusive kindness to both husband and wife.

The Useful Knowledge Society

NOTHING I AM ACQUAINTED WITH approaches so near to perfect happiness as the moment when knowledge, attended by her train of delightful tremors, steals in upon us. What emotion! What transcendent vibrations of the charmed mind. However, the following story illustrates the type of mind I sometimes had to deal with.

I founded the Useful Knowledge Society in Carluke in 1836. It included a small museum of fossils, antiquarian remains, and a limited number of books from my own collection.

I organised and led excursions to the local quarries to study geology. To anyone having a desire for geological pursuits, and anxious to learn, I was ever ready to give assistance.

On long winter nights I gave lectures on subjects like astronomy and electricity, designed to exercise an educational influence, and to assist in freeing the people from the bonds of Superstition.

Once, when lecturing on "The Planetary System", I stated that the fixed stars were larger than the Earth. A farm labourer, whose intelligence had been outraged by this statement, shouted out: 'How the hell can that be? There's nae room for them!'

VANITY

I WAS WALKING up the Bushelhead road one day with the Rev. James Anderson, Auld Licht Minister of Carluke.

A farmer's cart loaded with coals had stuck on the hill. The carter was lashing the resisting horse with his whip and rugging* at the reins in a vain effort to get the beast to start.

'Stop! Stop, my good man,' cried the portly minister, 'that's not the way to treat animals. They always respond to kindness.

'Now, come along,' he said to the horse, patting it on the neck and gently pulling the reins. 'Come along now! There's a good fellow.'

The horse never moved.

'Man! – ' I exclaimed, 'ye dinna† understand horses! That's no' the way to speak to them.'

I sprung forward with a wild shout and let loose a whole string of oaths and imprecations. The startled horse flung itself forward on its collar and dragged the cart to the top of the hill without stopping.

A while ago, I was vaccinating the child of two very ostentatious Auld Lichts who were convinced they were "of the Elect". They had some points in common with

---

* *rugging* tugging
† *dinna* do not

the precentor,* who only knew of two people who might claim a place among the Elect – himself and the Meenister† – and he had his doots‡ aboot the Meenister.

'Puir wee mannie!'§ I muttered, as I handled the child. 'Puir wee mannie! Born to be damned! Hellfire and brimstone forever and ever.'

'No, no, Doctor!' interrupted the father. 'Ye mauna‖ say that. Ye ken we hae the promise. Born of Christian parents – the covenant with the parents shall be fulfilled unto the children.'

I said: 'I admit the latter, but I deny the former!'

At a grand dinner in Braidwood House the guests were rather pompous. I supped only a portion of my soup and instructed the waiter to leave the plate on the table beside me.

As each course came round I removed a portion of it from my plate and placed it in the soup-plate. The guests watched furtively, but I offered no explanation. Occasionally, I stirred the mixture with my fork.

Towards the end of the dinner, to the surprise of my hosts, who knew I did not drink, I called for a glass of sherry. I poured the sherry also into the soup-plate, stirred it all up once more, and then proclaimed: 'Ladies and gentlemen, ye now see what ye have in your guts!'

"Weetchy" Will, who took his nickname from his farm, Whiteshaw, never missed family worship, but was

---

* *precentor* a man or woman, not necessarily clergy, who leads the singing in church
† *Meenister* Minister
‡ *doots* doubts
§ '*Puir wee mannie!*' Poor little man
‖ *mauna* must not

fond of a dram* and sometimes known to pray in a very loud voice. One evening I passed his house just as he brought his prayers to an audacious crescendo.

'Wull!' I shouted through the window, 'D'ye think your Maker's deef?'†

---

* *dram* a drink of liquor, esp. whisky
† *deef* deaf

THE THREE STREAMS

WITH THE ADVENT of mining operations and iron manufacture in Carluke about 1837, three clearly marked types populated the parish; each bound together by the traditions and associations of its hereditary occupation. These three types flowed alongside of one another like three streams that refused to coalesce.

In the sheltered valley of the Clyde, and in the little gills* which run off from it, were to be found the fruit growers – a colony of small holders, shrewd canny men, with a whimsical vein of humour which was apt to express itself in the form of practical joking.

The banks of the Clyde rise very steeply and, on the higher lands and moors, were to be found the dairy farmers and stock-raisers, a vigorous, strenuous race.

Then there were the miners and colliers, a race by themselves given to political and theological disputation.

The miners here (limestone and ironstone workers), in general, are a superior class to colliers, and come up to that of ordinary mechanics in every respect. Colliers, on the contrary, seem a peculiar people, – ignorant, superstitious, reckless, and profane.

There are, however, very marked exceptions; for I know not a few who will not find many equals in the ordinary sphere of life for uprightness of conduct,

---

* *gills* gullies

general information, and marked observance of the Christian precepts.

It is the misfortune of colliers to make large wages; for this alone seems to be the cause of their recklessness. The majority, great majority of them, are certainly poor indeed, – without money and without comfort. No care is taken by them to provide for the contingencies of life; and nothing is so common as to hear that they "never earn a penny not already eaten." This is too true with the many.

A great interest in their employer's success or welfare does not burden them; and it seems something like inflicting punishment to ask a single movement or act wherein their own immediate interest is not felt.

At the public works here, excellent homes are provided for the workmen; but cleanliness and in-door arrangements will not bear to be inquired into. Notwithstanding of this, the cottager who this year carried the premium for the best kept cottage – let us say it with emphasis – is a collier.

Drunkenness and early marriage among the greater number of colliers constitute the sum of much of their misery; and these follies are strongly ministered to by ignorance and example.

Education is not desired among them; at least it is not taken advantage of. Boys of eight and ten years of age, and, we blush to say it, sometimes girls, are taken by their parents into the pits to work, who at first have, if no more, tobacco and pipes as their reward. Every collier *must* smoke tobacco. While still young they have "served their time", and now, if not before, they must ape their betters, and get drunk on pay-nights.

Anon, though in utter ignorance, and still very young, each must follow his father and grandfather's example, and marry, perhaps, some girl immature like himself. Children are thenceforth prematurely issued into the world, necessarily of pitiable mental capacity, to live without instructors amid the worst examples, and ultimately, in all probability, to follow in the same round.

If the grocer and the dram-seller were to refuse giving credit to the colliers, and teach them to gain before they eat or even drink (condemnable though it be) the produce of labour, a feeling of greater independence and more honour would be instilled, which, at least, would be a gain; and if schools were planted at their doors, and a system of strict education pursued, much good would result.

Appalled by the squalor I saw, I resolved to meet the problem headlong. I believed cleanliness could be achieved at very little cost, and so devised an effective, if somewhat drastic, ploy to achieve it.

Whenever I found filthy blankets or clothes I would say nothing at the time, but wait until I met the offending householder in the street. Then, with a deliberately raised voice, I would present the person with a bar of soap and a severe lecture on the connection between dirt and disease. Needless to say, within a short time, the neatness and cleanliness of our houses were the talk of the surrounding countryside.

Shams

I CANNOT TOLERATE COMPLAINERS, and have no time for hypochondriacs.

One of my patients said to me: 'Oh, Doctor, I had an awfu' time o't last nicht.[*] My een never gaed the gither a' nicht.'[†]

'Neither did mine,' I said sternly.

'D'ye tell me that! Were ye badly too?'

'Not at all,' I replied, 'my nose was between them.'

Another hypochondriac cornered me on Kirkton Street and complained of a "sore throat".

I said: 'I'll look at it now. Shut your eyes, woman, open your mouth and put out your tongue.'

When she did so, I tiptoed away on my goloshes and whipped round the corner, leaving her standing in the street with her eyes shut and her tongue out.

On another occasion, I had a man making a nuisance of himself over a stomach complaint, asking for "a bottle" to cure it. I was convinced it was psychological in origin, so I gave him a bottle of brine.

I never saw him again.

---

[*] *awfu' time o't last nicht* awful time of it last night
[†] *een never gaed the gither a' nicht* eyes never met together all night

Then, there was a woman who "fainted" on High Street, just outside The Black Bull Inn. It seemed to me a very convenient place to develop a sudden need for "spirituous" comfort.

After examining the woman, I said to the people who had gone to her rescue: 'Just take her up to the Police Office.'

She immediately jumped up and ran towards the Carnwath road as fast as she could!

Young John Steuart, of Brownlee, took a hypochondriacal turn and began to imagine he was falling into consumption.

He described his symptoms out at Jollyfield and they persuaded him to come and see me.

I sized him up rapidly and after examining his tongue and sounding him thoroughly, I roared at him in an angry, threatening voice: 'Go home, Sir! You have a galloping consumption!' It nearly startled him out of his wits.

That was the last anyone heard of John Steuart's "symptoms".

GYROLEPIS RANKINII

To ME, there is something unspeakably pleasing in the contemplation of nature, whether in its broad or in its minuter aspects; and I can scarcely believe it possible that everyone does not participate to some degree in the same feelings.

I had my first experience of it when I was a boy of about thirteen years of age. Already, I had acquired the habit of collecting curiosities of all sorts, but had little knowledge of their nature.

One day, at a bookstall in Glasgow, I happened to look at Ure's *History of Rutherglen and East-Kilbride*, and saw in the book pictures of fossils similar to those in my own collection. I bought the book (price 1/-),[*] and thereupon began my lifelong interest in the subject.

As a young man I wandered among the gills and quarries of Carluke parish, hammer in hand, searching for pieces of coal or limestone imprinted with the outlines of primordial ferns or the bones of strange creatures that lived and died hundreds of millions of years ago.

The mining operations in Carluke exposed the old land and water deposits of the coal age, and of the older sea bottoms – both teeming with the vestiges of ancient forms of life.

---

[*] *1/-* one shilling

The Gairhills was my favourite hunting ground, where I collected numerous and grand specimens from the high beds of the carboniferous strata.

True, the animals and plants of the far-past ages are no longer in existence amongst us, but they are so far preserved as to yield a pleasing insight into the ways of the Author of creation in maturing the earth for our habitation.

For example, the forests and jungles of the old world are now our coal beds, the animals that peopled the ancient seas are now our lime beds, and the sands of antiquity are now our rocks.

In 1840 I heard that the British Association for the Advancement of Science planned to stage an exhibition in Glasgow to illustrate the geological structure of the West of Scotland.

Intrigued by the idea, I submitted a selection of fossils from my collection. Dr John Scouler arranged them beautifully on tables in the College library, catching the eye of a few local geologists.

The famous Swiss naturalist, Louis Agassiz, was at that time touring the principal museums of Europe. His masterwork *Recherches sur les Poissons Fossiles** had brought the ancient seas to life, with hundreds of vivid line drawings of prehistoric fishes.

Arriving in Glasgow, Professor Agassiz first visited the College to view the exhibition. On seeing my fossils his eyes lit up and he demanded to meet "Monsieur Rankine". I was introduced, and he embraced me with unfeigned enthusiasm and delight.

---

* *Researches on the Fossil Fishes*

PROFESSOR AGASSIZ
Courtesy of Wikimedia Commons

Suddenly scientists, and even laymen, were speaking of my specimens in breathless whispers! I was offered £300 for my collection, but declined to sell it.

Agassiz later revealed why he had been so excited. Referring to his Glasgow visit, he wrote:

> Mr. Rankine (sic) showed me so many new carboniferous specimens of that neighbourhood that I seemed to be handling a completely new formation.

He was astonished to find among my exhibits a new species: a large ray-finned fish with diamond-shaped scales and sculptured plates defending its head.

He later named this peculiar creature:

GYROLEPIS RANKINII

One human incident remains to be told of this meeting. On the final day, I was to read a paper on the geology of Carluke. But minutes before my name was called I was attacked by a fit of nerves.

I thrust my paper into the hands of a startled friend, begged him to read it on my behalf, jumped on my horse and fled for home!

REEKY LUMS

I WILL NOT TELL YOU how often I have watched and been amused by a human being about to perform the important act of taking a smoke. The smoker is an artist! We shall try a sketch.

The devotee first seats himself with something like dignity and gravity. The pipe is handled and looked at in a general way. It is now brought nearer his eyes, and a kind of exploration is conducted having special reference to the contents of the bowl.

Presently fingers fumble about the lower verge of the vest, and something is caught by the finger and thumb. The article turns out to be a small lever, which is very cleverly applied to remove some substance in the bottom of the pipe. The design seems to succeed, for the lever is replaced, and something like ashes is tumbled out. This, ladies and gentlemen, is the dottle!*

The empty pipe is now very artfully laid near the dottle, and both are surveyed with satisfaction. A dreamy sort of smile and look announce the completion of this stage of the process.

The right hand now seems to be commissioned to go in search of something deposited about the clothes, but there appears to be uncertainty as to the precise locality. It is nevertheless secured, and it turns out to be very

* *dottle* the plug of half-burnt tobacco left at the bottom of a pipe after smoking

like a tin-box. This is very carefully opened, and the end of a dark twisted substance projects from the half-closed lid, which is lengthened or shortened according to some understood rule and, with the thumb, nipped off. This, you must understand, is unburned tobacco, in such a state of impurity, as fitted the ends of the manufacturer.

This precious morsel is laid across the digits, and looked at approvingly. Part of the labour of the manufacturer is now reversed – the leaf is by the nice movement of both hands and both thumbnails, subjected to a tattering nipping.

The pipe is again lifted, applied to the lips, and air is sucked in and blown out. The numerous crumbs are now brought together and ingeniously huddled into the pipe – something after the fashion of loading a gun. It now appears evident that the dottle is not a rejected thing, for it is carefully placed on the top of the previous loading as if by way of priming. The business now seems ended. What more, indeed, need be done? Merciless artist! All this masterful manipulation goes for nothing!

A spunk* is struck into fiery activity, and crumbled dottle is ignited, the pipe is grasped by the teeth, and our devotee, with distorted face, upcast eyes, and restless lips, spews most barbarously in intermitting streams a most abominable, reeky† and sickening cloud upon the pure atmosphere, so openly and thoughtlessly, he ought in fairness be forced to swallow, or in failing that duty, should be sent to prison or to a place set aside for the purpose, like the leper houses of old!

---

* *spunk* spark
† *reeky* smoky

As a young man, James Forrest of The Yett (Willie's father), was never allowed to smoke at home, and even after he had left home, he never used to smoke in his father's house. He would go out into the garden, or take a walk along the road, whenever he wanted a whiff.

Once, when he was home on a visit, he brought with him a fine meerschaum pipe, which he was engaged in colouring. He took it out with him, and was quietly enjoying a puff by the road, when I came riding along on my black horse.

'Man, Jimmie,' I exclaimed, 'that's a braw* pipe ye've got! Let me have a look at it.'

Jimmie proudly handed over his treasure for my inspection.

I hurled it to the ground with such force that it was smashed to pieces. Then, snatching his staff, I tapped him on the head with it, and said: 'Man, if your Maker had meant you to smoke he wid† have made a lum‡ in your heid!'§

---

* *braw* good-looking
† *wid* would
‡ *lum* chimney
§ *heid* head

HYPOCRISY

REV. ANDERSON sometimes treated himself to a glass of toddy,[*] especially if he were feeling "no' weel".[†]

Once, when he was ailing, I found him sitting in his room with a glass of toddy. I told him: 'I can see you're on the road for Hell!' I turned and left the room.

Thomas Hobart, from Kirriemuir, succeeded James Anderson as Auld Licht minister.

One day, when I was in the manse, Rev. Hobart asked a very long grace before tea. I had a second cup of tea but left it sitting before me, untasted.

Hobart asked me: 'Is there anything wrong with your tea, Doctor?'

I said: 'I doot it's no as guid as the first, for I notice ye haven't asked grace on *it*.'

On one occasion, I was called urgently to a woman who had fainted, only to find the house full of gossiping neighbours. I bundled them all out without ceremony, and proceeded to examine the patient.

As I was leaving, one of the gossips, bolder than the rest, sidled up to me and asked confidentially: 'Is it anything serious, Doctor?' I put my mouth to her ear and whispered: 'Original Sin!'

---

[*] *toddy* a drink made by adding hot water and sugar to whisky
[†] "*no' weel*" not well

A while ago, a woman deposited half-a-crown on the corner of my desk and made for the door without saying a word. I called her back.

'What's that?' I said sternly.

'That's your fee,' she retorted. 'Ye tak' it frae ithers,[*] an'[†] what wey[‡] will ye no tak' it frae me?'

'Whae tell't ye that?' I asked.

'It was Mrs ———.'

'Did she say she paid me herself in this way?'

'She did.'

'Well, she's a liar, for she has never paid me. But I'll send her in a bill tonight!'

---

[*] *frae ithers* from others
[†] *an'* and
[‡] *wey* way

HIS WILD NATURE

I AM A MOST IMPATIENT READER. I have no toleration for anything but the old book of Nature. As I went my rounds through the country, birds, beasts and insects came under my watchful eye, their habits studied day by day until their life histories felt familiar.

For many years my special study was the slow-worm, a creature relatively abundant in Clydesdale. Despite its serpent-like appearance and motions (such as constantly darting out its long, partially-cleft tongue) this peculiar reptile is neither a snake – nor a worm – but a legless lizard. It feeds on slugs &c.,[*] found low in the grass, where too, from its mode of progression, it is most active and powerful.

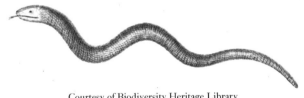

Courtesy of Biodiversity Heritage Library

Not venomous and, even if provoked, this shy animal will slither away and hide rather than bite a human – at least in no instance, during years of daily handling, did

---

[*] &c. and other (similar) things

I ever observe the slightest approach at defence by this mode.

Periodically, I sent anatomical specimens and reports of my observations to Dr Allen Thomson, who had taken over the Chair of Anatomy at Glasgow University after the death of Professor Jeffray in 1848. Thomson wrote to me in 1856, requesting skulls of various animals, to which I replied:

> You will receive skulls of newt, slowworm, weasel, ferret, opossum, shrew, fox, armadillo, agouti, rabbit, cat, &c.

In that year, my paper on the habits of the slow-worm was published in an Edinburgh scientific journal.

A friend gifted to me another member of the class *Reptilia* as a pet: a baby crocodile. I kept this native of a tropical clime in an enclosure in my back yard and, with great care, nursed him until he attained maturity. Occasionally, he would break out and terrorise the neighbours' bairns.[*]

One warm summer day, to satisfy my studious mind, I conveyed him out to the moor and released him into the "Cadger's Dub".[†] He had his liberty at last – but not for long! Lurking among the rushes, with only his snout and unblinking eyes poking out above the water, his wild nature re-asserted itself and, for safety's sake, he had to be shot.

I wasn't quite ready to let go of my unique companion, so I had him stuffed, and placed him in the vestibule at the foot of the stair that led to my rooms.

---

[*] *bairns* children
[†] *"Cadger's Dub"* hawker's pond

DEMON DRINK

I SHUDDER ALMOST to enter upon the subject of use and abuse of ardent spirits. Drunkenness is the result of the vilest and most un-natural habit which man has adopted. It is the mark under which he unmajestically struts before his Maker unabashed, and in his debasement plays fearful havoc to his own system, his home and his country.

It is a habit common among learned and unlearned, reaching even at times to Ministers of the Gospel and Magistrates. Alas, I doubt there can ever be a remedy. If drinking were abolished, the loss to the Exchequer would be too great. The useful employment of the officers of the law, from the Lord Advocate to the Hangman, would be lost!

A number of young men were carousing on the street corner near my house, leaning up against the wall and indulging in bad language. One night I went out and took my stand among them with my hands in my pockets and my back to the wall. I said not a word, but before long they began to slink away. Next night I came out as soon as they arrived, and they made off at once.

I consider sport harmful because it is invariably associated with heavy drinking. Recently I was present at a gathering where I chatted pleasantly with three young men. To the first, who was fond of painting, I described an attractive view, and where it was to be found. To the second, who was interested in geology, I indicated where certain fossils could be obtained. Finally, I came to a youth well known for his love of sport. I told him: 'The nearest public house is at Crossford.'

DANNY LONGLEGS

DANNY LONGLEGS" felt a pleasant kind of melancholy, and went to visit his favourite views and nooks,* feeling strangely that he would never see them again. He said nothing to anyone, but indulged his quite pleasant sadness. In the evening his father sent him off to recall a girl who had applied earlier in the day for a servant's job.

Danny always did things eagerly, so he rushed off, down past Cairdie's brig,† and up to Horsley hill, and so on to Overtown, where he found the girl in her house. On his way back, he suffered a palpitation of the heart so severe it frightened him, and he arrived completely done out.

A messenger was sent to fetch "the Doctor". So I got on my horse and galloped out along the Mauldslie Road to Brownlee House, where a small, dark-haired woman waited anxiously for me at the front door steps – Danny's mother Sarah.

Daniel Rankin Steuart – or "Danny Longlegs" – as I'd nicknamed him, was the second youngest of her twelve children. When he was born, all of the Steuart family names had been pretty well used up, so they named him after the family doctor – me!

---

* *nooks* small, sheltered places
† *Cairdie's brig* hawker's bridge

Danny had an accident in his early childhood, when the foot of a stool hit him with its full weight on his right eye. Afterwards he was weakly, and sensitive about his "gley'd een".*

Now a boy of twelve, he had been trying to build up his strength using his brothers' dumb-bells and swinging by the arms from branches of trees over the River Clyde. But the exertion had proved too much for him, and an enlargement of the heart had developed.

I prescribed digitalis to control his heart rate: 'Ten drops night and morning, increasing drop by drop.' He used it until his hands and feet got blue, and then he stopped for a few days.

One night he had another bad attack and everybody thought the end had come. But at the worst stage he had a vision of Jesus above him bending down to receive him in his arms. This calmed him, and he waited to see what would happen.

Gradually, he began to feel right again, but thereafter he had a nervous terror of being left alone, and his mother was just as nervous about leaving him.

I ordered Danny out of school. His cousin, who was training to be a doctor, tutored him at home. He remained troubled by heart palpitations, and dared not read an exciting novel, knowing he might die suddenly. Confined to the house, he was gazing out of the window one day when he saw an old gangrel† wife going past with her barrow, all alone and without fear. He looked at her with envy, but he was never low-spirited.

Thanks to careful nursing by his mother he slowly recovered, and, as he got stronger, he started going out

---

* *"gley'd een"* squinted eyes
† *gangrel* vagrant

for short walks, accompanied by his mother and supported by a staff.

Then one summer he was sent for a change to Rothesay with his older brother Jamie. It had a miraculous effect: he threw away his staff on the second day. The old castle, the ships, and the hills were a delight, and he made drawings of his favourite places and scenes.

I encouraged him to take up an interest in Botany. His brothers, who belonged to the Useful Knowledge Society, borrowed books for him to read. He studied William Patrick's *The Flora of Lanarkshire* and made out the names of all the common plants for himself without any other help.

He delighted in beauty, and began to wander alone about the woods and orchards, revelling in the splendour of the valley. He had favourite spots from which to enjoy the outlook from the house.

The "Green" was a large plot of grass, the width of the house, which sloped gently for two or three hundred yards towards the Clyde. In it were clumps of daffodils and, at the sides, two rows of ancient trees. The ground then fell steeply, afterwards less steeply, until it reached the river half a mile away.

The Clyde here is fifty to a hundred yards wide, and sweeps round Dalserf Holm, a level peninsula of about a hundred acres with its kirk and kirkyard at the isthmus, and orchards, villages, farms and gentlemen's seats on the slope on the other side of the valley.

When the river comes down in spate, it fills the valley with a loud rushing sound. But when all the sounds are hushed, its gentle murmuring can soothe the soul.

For several years Danny's health remained delicate, and knowing he was not expected to live, he was afraid to hope.

But he continued to wander about the braes,* nourishing his youth sublime with the fairy tales of science and the long results of time. And eventually he began to harbour again the big hopes and ambitions common to all youth.

One day, he thought, if he lived, he might become something great.

---

* *braes* hills

Drawing Teeth

OF ALL THE ABOMINABLE THINGS I have to do as a doctor, the one to which I have the most violent antipathy is drawing teeth.

I was just mounting my horse to go out on a visit when an old woman came up to me. She had a shawl tied round her jaw, which was knotted at the top of her head.

'Oh Doctor, my tooth is rotted! Ye maun[*] tak' it oot. I'm fair desperate wi' it.'

After examining the tooth I told her: 'I'm too busy today, my good woman. Away along to Doctor Cullen and he'll pull it for you.'

'Oh Doctor, I've just been along to him, but I've only got a sixpence and he'll no pull it for less than a shillin'.'

'Here,' I said, handing her another sixpence, 'awa' an' mak'[†] him tak' it oot!'

Another patient who needed a tooth pulled caught me at home. I left the room for a few minutes and returned with a large rope, which I laid out on the table.

After another look at the tooth, I went out again and returned with a very large basin, which I placed on the floor. Then I went out and fetched a large hammer and

---

[*] *maun* must
[†] *mak'* make

chisel, and a pair of blacksmith's tongs, which I laid on the table, beside the rope.

I examined the tooth once more, muttering to myself and shaking my head gloomily. A fourth time I left the room, but when I returned my study was empty!

The patient had fled.

An old lady visited my surgery to get a tooth pulled. I climbed up on the back of the chair on which she was sitting, and yelled in a fearsome voice: 'Open your mouth!' She got such a fright she jumped up, the chair toppled over and I fell my full length on the floor. However, as I'd suspected, the fright put away her toothache.

George Brown, whose father was gardener at Orchard House, met me in the street. He was suffering terribly from the toothache.

'I called on several doctors but they were all out,' he said, adding: 'can you no' pull it for me, Doctor?'

I said: 'Man, I don't like drawing teeth. But if you're terrible bad I'll try my hand.'

I took him up to my room. I had none of the pincers or fancy appliances dentists use nowadays. My only instrument was an old-fashioned key, like that used for screwing on nuts. If the tooth wasn't big enough to catch the key, I just wrapped a bit of paper round it.

I got the key into George's mouth and set to work with it, levering the tooth up. It was something of an experience I can tell you! By and by, I got the tooth lifted up about half way out of the socket.

'Now,' I said, 'that's a good beginning. I'll have to take a rest.'

With that, I sat down in my chair and looked at George for about five minutes. He wasn't able to shut his mouth because of the big tooth sticking up.

'Now,' I said, 'you've stood it very well,' and I took hold of the tooth again. It came away quite easily.

'How much is there to pay?' said George.

'Pay!' I cried, 'there's nothing to pay. I never charged for drawing a tooth yet.'

'Well,' he said, 'there's a shillin' anyway.'

I shoved it back to him.

'Put that in your pouch,' I said. 'When you go to the Kirk next Sunday you can put sixpence in the plate, and you can spend the other sixpence on yourself. Only don't buy tobacco with it.'

DARWIN'S BULLDOG

THOMAS HUXLEY was known as "Darwin's Bulldog" for championing the famous English naturalist's controversial Theory of Evolution, which had caused uproar in church circles.

In 1860, Huxley clashed with the Bishop of Oxford, Samuel Wilberforce, who was a fierce opponent of the idea that Man was descended from the apes.

In a heated exchange, Wilberforce asked Huxley if he was descended from an ape on his mother's side, or his father's side? Huxley shot back that he would rather be descended from an ape than a bishop!

Afterwards this witty riposte was widely reported in pamphlets, and even a spoof play.

Young Huxley had a mind quite brilliant. Despite a lack of private means, he made good through the force of his tenacious personality.

Aged 20, and deeply in debt, he launched a scientific career on the back of discoveries about marine life he had made during a four-year long Naval expedition to New Guinea and Australia. Such a man is stopped by nought – well, almost!

Huxley began his correspondence with me in 1862, seeking permission to examine specimens of fossil fishes in my collection. At the time he was lecturer in Natural History at the Government School of Mines in London.

After inviting him to Carluke, I received the following letter, at which I find myself laughing yet:

"January 16, 1862."

I did my best to reach Carluke on the 5th of this month – stopping for that purpose at Carstairs on the 4th – and hoping to be able to spend two or three hours over your collection by taking the early train from Carstairs which stops at Carluke. But arriving at Carstairs very late and very hungry in consequence of the bad arrangements of the railway people I was misguided enough to eat the only food the good landlady could offer – to wit – a "welsh rabbit" – which vile and detestable effort of cookery was very nearly the death of me – a circumstance which your medical experience will lead you to understand and which mine, small as it is, ought to have taught me to anticipate.

The result of this contretemps was that I was physically incapacitated from starting at the hour I intended, and as I was obliged to reach Forfar (?) that night I was compelled to renounce all hope of seeing your collection. On some future occasion however when I certainly shall not put up at Carstairs, I hope to have the pleasure of availing myself of your kind permission.

Ay, it took Carstairs Junction to impale "Darwin's Bulldog"!

SANNIE BASIL

S ANNIE BAUSIL" – his real name was Alexander Basil
Steuart – is said to have belonged to a branch of the
Steuarts of Murdostoun and Allanton. It is said also
that he was in the direct succession of the small estate of
Brownlie, near Orchard, but that his father, who was
weak-witted like himself, had sold his right of
succession to a cousin for an annuity. While his father
was alive he lived with him at Steuart Hall near The
Holm at Orchard, where there were a lot of little
lairdships.

Sannie's most strongly marked characteristic was
laziness. It was said of him that if he were on fire he
would not shake the sparks off himself. And sure
enough, when the house actually caught fire, he was too
lazy to rise from his bed. He shouted to the children:
'Rin* an' tell Poplar (Cunningham, of Poplarhill, a
neighbour) the hoose is on fire – an' me lyin' in my
bed!'

Mr Stevenson, the Laird of Braidwood, once caught
Sannie cutting "souples"† in his wood.

'Hullo Sannie!' he exclaimed. 'What the Deevil do
you mean by cutting souples on my ground?'

'It was Forrest o' The Heids that sent me oot to cut
them,' said Sannie. 'I'm to get 3/- for the day's work.'

---

* *Rin* Run
† "*souples*" long strips of bark used to make hinges for flails

'Ay,' said the Laird, 'but he didna' tell you to steal them.'

'Fine he kent, Laird,' was the reply, 'I had nae woods o' my ain.'[*]

Steuart, of Brownlee, was very kind to old Sannie. On one occasion he sent him a bag of oatmeal. As the carter brought it into the house he stumbled against the doorpost and the sack fell from his back.

'Never mind,' said Sannie, 'let it lie there; we'll jist tak' it in as we need it.' So there it lay. The children used to pour a little water into the sack and make "crowdie"[†] for themselves.

After the death of his father, Sannie built a small divot[‡] house on the moor, and there he lived by himself.

Forrest of The Yett and I were once overtaken by a very heavy shower, and took refuge in Sannie's little hut. We found him sitting in the middle of the floor sheltering under an umbrella from the rain, which was coming in by a hole in the roof.

'Why don't you mend your roof, Sannie?' I exclaimed.

'Ye wad na' hae me gang oot[§] in this weather to mend it!' protested Sannie.

'Well, why don't you go out and mend it when it's fine weather?' I asked.

'But there's nothing the matter wi' it then!' said Sannie.

---

[*] *ain* own
[†] *"crowdie"* a porridge of oatmeal and water
[‡] *divot* turf
[§] *Ye wad na' hae me gang oot* You wouldn't have me go out

HUNTER OF "THE DALES"

JOHN HUNTER is known as a great antiquarian collector and, between him and I, there was considerable rivalry.

In the spring of 1868, when Hunter had just turned 33, he set out for America, and travelled through a large part of the "Wild West", having the honorary degrees of LL.D. and D.Sc.[*] conferred upon him by the University of Philadelphia in recognition of his scientific labours. He used to tell of an experience he had when in America, with General Morgan, one of the leaders in the War of Secession.

Both were staying in a Kansas hotel at the same time, and on one occasion a heated discussion arose between them on the war, which so tried the temper of the American that, in a moment of passion, he was about to resort to the use of his revolver.

Hunter, foreseeing the probable course of events, already had the advantage of his opponent, and his cool and plucky response caused the latter to retire in confusion.

Next day, the General apologised to Hunter, complimenting him for his real British pluck. 'Scottish,' replied Hunter, correcting him as they shook hands heartily.

---

[*] *LL.D. and D.Sc.* Doctor of Laws and Doctor of Science

HUNTER OF "THE DALES"
Courtesy of the Geological Society of Glasgow

Soon after his return from America, Hunter joined in partnership with Dr John Selkirk, the wealthy owner of the Braidwood Coal, Lime, and Coke Company and, as he had a colliery manager's certificate signed by the Secretary of State for Scotland, he acted as manager for the company.

Not long after he started work, a new rope had been placed on the drum at the pithead for winding purposes. The first person thereafter sent down was an Irishman; by an oversight, the engineman forgot to uncoil the rope, with the result that the unlucky son of Erin descended the shaft with the speed of a plummet. He escaped, however, with a few bruises and a shake to his nerves.

When the man's wounds had been attended to and some "spirituous" comfort administered, the alarm subsided, and the doctor resumed conversation with a friend. The Irishman was reclining within earshot and, overhearing allusion made to a Bible four hundred years old, which the doctor himself had bought, he raised his head, fixed a pair of wondering eyes upon his employer, and asked in awe-struck tones: 'Faith, Doctor, and did yez buy it when it was new?'

About this time, Hunter married Dr Selkirk's sister, Mary, who was 58 years of age. One of the neighbours remarked: 'I dinna wonder at that. He was aye* fond o' auld tings!'†

When Hunter first married, he lived at Midloan. He then purchased the estate of Daleville. The house known as "The Dales" is a plain but commodious country mansion on the right bank of the Clyde, a short walk from Ha'-bar.‡ He had a brass plate affixed to his front door announcing himself as "Dr John Hunter".

Shortly after this plate had been put up, I rode up to his house to call on him. I studied the plate for a moment, then tethered my horse and made my way round to the back door on which I hammered loudly.

'Dear me, Doctor,' exclaimed Mrs Hunter. 'What are you doing round here? Did you try the front door?'

'Yes,' I said, 'I was at the front door, but I see some stranger has come to stop there – some "Doctor Hunter" whom I never heard tell of before!'

---

* *aye* always
† *tings* things
‡ *Ha'-bar* Hallbar tower

Standing on My Head

MY OLDER SISTER MAGGIE, a wee, wizened woman of 73, to whom I am much attached, keeps house for me.

Every morning, on a plain wooden table without a tablecloth, she lays out my wholesome breakfast of porridge, buttermilk, eggs and scones – the only meal I take during the day.

With old age creeping up on me, I've taken up yoga, and regularly can be found standing on my head in the corner of my surgery. When executing this feat I remove all my outer garments and retain only my underclothes, in the style of a Yogi. It's somewhat embarrassing for my visitors but an excellent way to get rid of the ones I don't like.

After years of practice among the poor I've acquired great proficiency in shaving people. During an illness, Mr Harvie, the laird of Brownlee, complained of the irritation of his beard, and I promptly removed it for him. He praised my skill, and expressed surprise at this unusual attention. I replied: 'There is a great Example you know.'

One woman, having heard of the efficacy of my pills, begged me for a box. I promised her one and, next time I was passing, handed her a pill-box. Inside was half-a-sovereign. She needed nourishment, not medicine.

A neighbouring farmer adopted an orphan in her childhood. When she grew up she had a long severe illness, during which I attended on her. For my services I declined to accept any payment, in spite of persistent offers by the farmer. Finally, I said: 'You did not tell me, Jock, that Mary was a foundling.'

'She's nae foundling,' replied the farmer.

'O yes, she is!' I continued. 'You've fed and clad her, Jock. I'll doctor her.'

I signed medical certificates simply, as would a priest or layman. One of my certificates was presented to the Sheriff, who accepted it, but later sent me a polite letter pointing out it was legally essential for doctors to affirm all certificates on the basis of "soul and conscience." In reply, I thanked the Sheriff for his kindness, but added:

> As I know nothing of the soul, or of the conscience, the bench would, perhaps, accept certificates in future vouched on the basis of "heart and liver", both of which I have often examined, and somewhat understand.

A man considered by many the most enthusiastic fossil hunter in Scotland called at my house asking for directions to Gair and Westerhouse, which he proposed to visit that day. In conversation, it transpired he had already visited Brockley and Lesmahagow, then walked across to Carluke. I exclaimed: 'Sir, your name is "Armstrong"[*] – it ought to be "Legstrong"!'

---

[*] "*Armstrong*" James Armstrong, co-founder in 1858 of the Geological Society of Glasgow

BLUNT BOB

THE MIDDLE WARD OF CLYDESDALE, which commences at the junction of the Nethan with the Clyde, is a district of the most splendidly beautiful and fertile character.

The several miles of which it consists, along the banks of the river, are one uninterrupted series of grove, garden, and orchard. It is quite unlike every other part of Scotland – a billowy ocean of foliage, waving in the summer wind, and glowing under the summer sun!

The people of the Upper Ward call this magnificent region, "the Fruit Lands"; and well is it worthy of the appellation. Fruit is here produced on a scale of profusion, of which strangers can have no idea. It overhangs the roads and the waters, bobs against the head of the passing traveller, and dips in the rushing stream.

"Orchard" is a small estate in the very centre of the Fruit Lands. Orchard House stands upon the southern slopes of an isolated hill called "the Swinstie", opposite Crossford, and commanding a beautiful prospect towards Craignethan Castle.

Behind the Swinstie, nestling among apple, pear, and plum trees, is the smallholding of Gowanglen. There, some ninety years ago, a certain Robert Scott had a nursery garden. He did a considerable business in supplying the orchards of the Clyde with fruit trees, and his fame was established as a fruit-bud grafter and pruner.

In 1789, Robert married Agnes Lindsay, and in 1808 they had a son, also named Robert. The son succeeded the father in Gowanglen, and when he grew up, he married Mary, daughter of "Boatie" Thomson, the ferryman at Crossford.

In 1831, Robert and Mary had a son, also named Robert. When this grandson, whom the family called "Bob", grew up, he became known as a terrible man for making fun of people. He was "gey* blunt" and could give people a "very hard nip".

Bob's uncle, John Scott, had a wife who died in 1872. Nine months later, he planned to remarry. He was 57, and his bride-to-be was 33. Her hair had already begun to turn grey, and she told her future husband not to ask "Blunt Bob" to the wedding.

However, after the marriage, on the first Sunday the newly-weds went to church, Bob walked behind them until he met up on them just at the church door.

'There's been a great deal of talk,' he said, 'about the difference of ages, but I'll be whippet† if I can tell which o' ye has the advantage!'

I was the family's doctor, but never sent in any bill for my services. I simply ordered a basket of fruit, with me never to pay, so the account was kept fairly balanced. One day "Blunt Bob" came to consult me about some affection of his skin.

I took his hand and examined it carefully, then with a concerned look said: 'Man, Robert, do you know of

---

* "*gey*" very
† *whippet* whipped

any place round here where they send lepers?'

Bob shuddered, as if a cauld* shiver had run right through him. He said: 'D'ye think it's leprosy, Doctor?'

'I don't like it,' I said, shaking my head, 'but hand me a bit o' paper and I'll write ye out a prescription. There, get a pennyworth o' that, and I think it'll cure ye!'

---

* *cauld* cold

A Thing of Beauty

I<small>T'S BEEN FORTY YEARS</small> since I became custodian of the relics of John Greenshields, sculptor of *The Jolly Beggars*. It's those "scandalous" statues of his I'm going to tell you about. But, before I do, I have yet another sin to confess.

Here, in my study, the shelves all round are filled with skulls, and bones, and fossils, and books, but one thing I covet more than all the others, and I will not part with it until the day I die.

I often talked to John of the difficulty of representing sleep and infantile form, and I pressed on him one or other of these subjects, in every way different from anything he had yet attempted.

'Why not both in one,' he replied, as if his mind had already been directed to the subject.

He had, indeed, been contemplating something of the kind, and presented a design in oil of a sleeping child which he had procured; but he was easily persuaded that the design was useless for his purpose, and needed little urging to study from the living form.

He warmed to the idea at once; and, soon after, started to discover and study all the infantile population within reach. The enthusiasm with which he prosecuted this subject exceeded in degree anything previously observed in his career; for, in general, his designs seemed to take form intuitively.

A plump, well-thriven child, aged about twelve months, was ultimately selected for a model, which he resolved to transfer to the clay without altering a line.

He worked from memory and measurements in the first instance, but the child was brought to him for the finishing touches – stript, put to sleep, and placed in position: a perfect copy was produced.

I was summoned, and a long scrutiny was made of the clay model. The form was beautiful, and seemed to be without fault, – still we hung over the figure, giving slight touches till enough of daylight was scarcely left for preparing the stucco and enveloping the clay towards forming a mould. Next day a cast was taken.

No cold inanimate form could come nearer life. The beautiful design was never transferred to stone, although the artist was prouder of this simple effort than of any more complicated production of his hands. To this day, I keep it always so placed as to meet my eye – "a thing of beauty."

The other day twa[*] farmers stopped me in the street. I tried to jink[†] past them as if I was late for an appointment. But these days I'm an old man. Not so quick on my feet. They'd come to me to get a sight o' *The Jolly Beggars.* I keep them under lock and key out at Kirkton House. That's the safest place for them. The old manor house is empty and no one dares go there after dark. Major Weir, "the Warlock", was born and brought up at Kirkton. He was burned for sorcery, and that has burdened the place with a stigma. His spirit still hovers there!

I returned to my house to get the key and, knowing

---

[*] *twa* two
[†] *jink* dodge

how strongly I disapprove of the demon drink, the farmers took advantage of my absence to get a dram at the public house.

On seeing *The Jolly Beggars*, they exclaimed in admiration at their realistic nature and, one of them, pointing to the figure of the "raucle carlin",* remarked:

'That yin† looks as if she could tak' her dram!'

'Ay,' I said, sniffing the air, 'An' I can smell it off the jaud‡ yet!'

Mr. John Young,
Under-keeper of the Hunterian Museum

Dear Sir, Do you give any space to works of art in your museum? I have at my disposal the original models of the Jolly Beggars (8 figures about 18 inches high) no copy of which exist in lifesize. Some forty years ago they were the rage of the time. Before looking elsewhere, I shall wait till I hear from you and then I can or not offer them.

At pages 311-12 of the book§ I send for your acceptance (<u>private</u>) you will see a notice of the "Jolly Beggars". I am

Yours sincerely
DR Rankin
9 April 1875

---

* "*raucle carlin*" fat hag
† *yin* one
‡ *jaud* hussy
§ Anon. [Rankin], *Notices*

MAGGIE

M AGGIE DIED.[*] The next morning I sent for Bob Pettigrew, the joiner, and gave him an order to make a coffin six feet long and two feet wide. He stared at me, and said: 'Your sister is dead, I hear. Had I not better measure her?'

'No,' I said, 'make the coffin as I tell you.'

When the coffin arrived, I pointed to the side of the door and said: 'Let it down there, Bob.'

'But how about the kistin'?'[†]

'Oh, I'll see to that.'

That night I kisted the body myself, and put all her clothes and shoes into the coffin. It was a simple, box-like affair, covered with plain black cloth, no mounting or gilded gear.

At the funeral everyone was surprised at its size.

The ceremony was conducted in private, with no display or ostentation; all parade prevented in every way. No gingerbread.

All these things I disapproved of.

---

[*] *Maggie died* Saturday, 3 June 1876
[†] *kistin'(g)* the swathing of a corpse in plain woollen cloth

A WIDOW FRIENDSHIP

I RECEIVED A NOTE FROM MARION. Her husband had passed away, leaving her a widow. I cautioned her:

My Dear Marion,

Letters are neither good nor safe — handed about as they are, and bought and sold, and stuck into albums, and turned to all manner of vulgar uses.

Yet, despite this warning, the friendship that had ended so abruptly 45 years earlier, sparked back to life. My letter continued . . .

In our day great progress has been made in tempering the mind to truth — as truth can be discerned — amounting to something like a series of revolutions. Much that I dreamt about and even predicted has come.

Nature, strictly interpreted, has yielded grand results, and given the finest lessons. To record these, in purity, is one mission of man, and by doing so the dross of ignorance — a sort of poison — may be washed away.

God — the Creator — the sustainer of all things, must come to be more and more recognised and worshipped. Superstition, amongst all septs, shall wither and die.

Tennyson says somewhere –

"the worst that follows
Things that seem'd jerk'd out of the common rut
Of Nature – is the religious fool"

– who is ready to fight and die for an idea he could never comprehend. Warfare of this sort, how awful. Understandable things are alone valuable to man.

Ever affectionately yours
D.R. Rankin
5 February 1877

DANNY RETURNS

M Y LEGS ARE GETTING WEAKLY NOW, and I had to cling to the furniture for support as I walked to the door. When I saw who it was, I saluted him gleefully: 'Danny Longlegs!'

I was leaning on the door-handle, so couldn't take his hand at first. But as soon as he was in and I'd got myself balanced, I said: 'Where's your hand now, Dan?' and gave it a kindly shake.

We stood in the lobby for a minute while I showed him some specimens. He said: 'I'm afraid of keeping you too long standing on your feet!' I got out with a loud guffaw, and laughed: 'I've given up standing on my head now!'

Danny, at 31 years old, was 6 feet 8 inches tall. Chief Chemist of the Broxburn Oil Company, no less!

He had met a very pretty young woman called Maggie, and had serious designs on marrying her. That pleased me greatly.

We sat down and talked for two hours. I told him all sorts of interesting things of the snails, and the toads, and the frogs . . .

* * *

A few months after Danny's visit I suffered an attack of apoplexy that left me paralysed.

As the winter of my life advanced, I gradually withdrew from society and all social intercourse, as does the snail in its shell at the close of Autumn. And like it, I felt disposed to seal up the opening. So, when Rev. Hobart called and offered to pray for me, I declined.

'I know that many are praying for you,' said Hobart, to which I replied: 'They might be better employed, or they might be worse.'

My brain is as sharp as ever, although not quite as sharp as long ago, but I'm failing sadly in strength. Time has changed to silver the hair that once shone like gold. I've sent a letter to John Young at the Hunterian offering my collection of geological specimens – mostly fish remains.

Courtesy of Dr Peter J. Gordon

Dinner With The Deil

A TERRIFIC GALE broke out over the country on Monday[*] night. The evening began calm and mild, but a fresh wind set in, and heavy rain began to fall about eleven o'clock. The full fury of the storm may be said to have fairly begun at midnight. The wind was high, and the rain still poured. About two o'clock in the morning there was more wind and a good deal of lightning in the sky. An hour later it was the most severe storm we had experienced for a great many years.

At daybreak there was a heavy pounding on my front door. I ignored it. The pounding came again, this time more insistent. I heaved myself up off the bed and rose unsteadily to my feet. Clinging to a chair for support, I reached the door and opened it.

It was Rev. Hobart! But not the dignified man I knew. His clothes were dishevelled, and his face was etched with desperation. I admitted him at once.

With his eyes boring into mine, he said: 'We haven't much time. The manse window has been blown in. You must listen to me. Will you let me pray for your immortal soul?!'

For an instant I failed to grasp his meaning. But then, before my very eyes, a grisly vision loomed up.

---

[*] *Monday* 21 November 1881

I saw myself roasting in a huge witch's cauldron and, beside it, a great towzie tyke,[*] grim as Hell and black as coal, licked its lips – The Deil[†] himself!

I quickly nodded my assent to Hobart, and when his brief ceremony was over, I held out my hand . . .

---

[*] *towzie tyke* unkempt dog
[†] *Deil* Devil

Morning Sunrise

THE BRIGHTNESS OF MORNING SUNRISE, once a delight, has become a burden.

My funeral should be conducted as was that of my sister. Afterwards let the place of rest of the dead be undisturbed by headstone or monument, the grave yard being distinction enough.

DANIEL REID RANKIN

The Hamilton Advertiser
25 March, 1882

Death of Dr Rankin, Carluke

Daniel Reid Rankin died at his residence here, on the morning of the 21st inst.,[*] a few minutes past seven o'clock. In December, 1879, he had had an attack of paralysis by which he was prostrated for several months. He rallied a little in the summer season, and was even able at times to drive out, but the repeated recurrence of the disease precluded all hope of his final recovery, though he continued to enjoy occasional intervals of convalescence till near the end. Throughout his long illness he manifested great patience, and lost very little of his wonted[†] cheerfulness.

In the death of Dr Rankin, Carluke feels a loss. Being a man not only of lofty talent, but of a most amiable and obliging disposition, he was universally beloved; at the same time a man of high integrity and noble principle, one whose memory will be long cherished.

---

[*] *inst.* of the present month
[†] *wonted* customary

Notes and Sources

The "Auld Lichts"

7   *Every time*: Gordon, 'How oddly', 6
corner: Steuart, 104
Tuesday, 26th of March 1805: National Records of Scotland. Old Parish Registers Births 629/ Carluke 10/284
son of James and Isobel Rankin: NRS. Old Parish Registers Marriages 629/ Carluke 20/305
working class folk: Gray, 277
souter: Steuart, 103
Auld Licht: Gordon, 'How oddly', 3
religious: Steuart, 103
daughter of John Reid: NRS. Old Parish Registers Births 629/ Carluke 10/147
lively: Steuart, 104

8   *my father's workshops*: Martin, 2
existence of Hell: Burnett, 18
"cutty-stool": Ramsay, 26
Sabbath: Steuart, 104
when I was five: Gordon, 'How oddly', 1

9   *refused to go to church*: Gray, 281
impatience: Steuart, 115
comments: Ibid., 116
"hellish Dan": Ibid.
unorthodox views: Ibid., 138

Kay's School

10   *parish school*: Anon. [Rankin], 115
head of the High Street: MacCallum Scott, 'Writings', University of Glasgow Archives & Special Collections. GB 247 MS Gen 1465/518, 56
National Bank: Ibid.
Walston: Anon. [Rankin], 118
scholar: Ibid., 115
umbrella: Ibid.

11   *sprinkling of irony*: Ibid., 119

12   *a line from Virgil*: *The Eclogues*, Eclogue I, 1
moleskin jacket: Steuart, 107
baited: Ibid.
wild boars: Ibid.
"Danny, the devil": MacCallum Scott, 'Writings', 56

AN OBJECT OF INTEREST

MARION

21 *medical lectures*: Maclachlan and Stewart, 169
    distant relations: Steuart, 136–138

A LICENCE TO PRACTISE

24 *assistant to Robert Hunter*: Steuart, 108
    graduated: Addison, *Graduates*, 279
    appointed Professor: Duncan, 185
    absent: Steuart, 108
    licence: Royal College of Physicians and Surgeons of Glasgow,
    'Licentiate Register (1829)'. E-mail to the author, 10 October 2022
    promising post: Steuart, 108

25 *doctor's practice*: Ibid.

DOCTOR DAN

26 *In 1830*: Steuart, 110
    mansions: Ibid.
    settled down: Ibid.
    gifted: MacCallum Scott, 'Writings', 62
    horse: Steuart, 109
    threw me: MacCallum Scott, 'Writings', 62
    mode of dress: Steuart, 110
    tall-looking gent: Ibid., 109
    particular: Ibid.

27 *hair*: Ibid.
    brow: Ibid.
    'Doctor Dan': Ibid., 113
    front view: The Carluke and Lanark Gazette, 5 March 1926, 2f

28 *face*: Steuart, 109
    To children: Ibid., 112
    young Agnes: NRS. Census 1841, 629/ Carluke 4/1
    wheel of fashion: MacCallum Scott, *Clydesdale Man*, 36

HOUSE CALLS

29 *castle to cot*: MacCallum Scott, *Clydesdale Man*, 33
    never knocked: Ibid., 36
    wall: Ibid.
    infant: Ibid.

30 *poker*: MacCallum Scott, *Clydesdale Man*, 39
    'my card': Ibid., 36
    'horse-shoe nails': Ibid., 37
    'oatmeal poultice': Ibid.

MEANNESS

32 *without fee*: Steuart, 110
    wealthy lady: MacCallum Scott, *Clydesdale Man*, 39
    lingered: Steuart, 111

33 *miserly son*: Ibid.
    "Brew": MacCallum Scott, *Clydesdale Man*, 42

ENVIOUS TONGUES

35 *note from Marion*: Steuart, 138
    haemorrhage: Ibid.

36 *married*: Ibid., 139

THE USEFUL KNOWLEDGE SOCIETY

37 *perfect happiness*: Steuart, 117
    1836: Gordon, *New Statistical Account*, 594
    quarries: Steuart, 119
    desire: The Hamilton Advertiser, 25 March 1882, 1e
    lectures: Steuart, 114
    'nae room': Ibid., 133

VANITY

38 *resisting horse*: MacCallum Scott, *Clydesdale Man*, 42
    Auld Lichts: Ibid., 41

39 *grand dinner*: MacCallum Scott, 'Writings', 47
    "Weetchy Will": MacCallum Scott, *Clydesdale Man*, 41

THE THREE STREAMS

41 *mining operations*: Steuart, 110
    clearly marked types: MacCallum Scott, *Clydesdale Man*, 27
    colliers: Rankin, D.R. 'Sketch of the Geology of Carluke Parish,
    Lanarkshire'. In Anon. *Prize-Essays and Transactions of the Highland
    and Agricultural Society of Scotland*. Vol. XIV. 1843, 98–99

43 *soap*: Steuart, 111

SHAMS

44 *complainers*: Martin, 3
    'awfu' time': MacCallum Scott, *Clydesdale Man*, 37
    'Shut your eyes': Steuart, 111
    bottle: Martin, 3

45 *"fainted"*: Ibid.
    Young John Steuart: MacCallum Scott, 'Writings', 35

GYROLEPIS RANKINII

46 *contemplation of nature*: Steuart, 119
    experience: Ibid., 117
    wandered: Ibid., 119
    coal age: Ibid., 118

47 *Gairhills*: The Hamilton Advertiser, 25 March 1882, 1e
    animals: Steuart, 119
    exhibition: Ibid.

Dr John Scouler: Ibid.
Louis Agassiz: Ibid., 120
embraced: Ibid.

48 'Professor Agassiz': Antoine Sonrel, from his lithograph, mid-19th century
de.wikipedia.org/wiki/Louis_Agassiz#/media/Datei:Louis_Agassiz-2.jpg
£300: Steuart, 120
new formation: Agassiz, 36
plates: Young, 72

49 *named*: Steuart, 120
human incident: Ibid.
paper: Rankin, 'Sketch of the Geology of Carluke Parish, Lanarkshire'

REEKY LUMS

50 *The smoker*: Steuart, 141–142

51 *prison*: Martin, 4

52 *James Forrest of The Yett*: MacCallum Scott, *Clydesdale Man*, 40
'lum': Ibid., 39

HYPOCRISY

53 *glass of toddy*: MacCallum Scott, *Clydesdale Man*, 40
tea: Ibid., 41
'Original Sin!': Ibid.

54 *half-a-crown*: Ibid., 39

HIS WILD NATURE

55 *impatient reader*: Steuart, 118
special study: Ibid., 113
relatively abundant: Rankin, Daniel R. 'On the Structure and Habits of the
Slow-Worm', 26 November 1856. In Anon. *Proceedings of the Royal
Physical Society of Edinburgh (1854–1858)*, Vol. I. 1858, 191
tongue: Ibid., 188
slugs: Ibid., 184
'L'Orvet': Lacepède, Pl.21, 590
bite: Rankin, 'On the Structure and Habits of the Slow-Worm', 183–184

56 *anatomical specimens*: Steuart, 113
taken over the Chair: Murray, 245
skulls: Steuart, 113
paper: Rankin, 'On the Structure and Habits of the Slow-Worm'
crocodile: Steuart, 113
terrorise: Ibid.
Cadger's Dub: The Carluke and Lanark Gazette, 5 March 1926, 2f

DEMON DRINK

57 *I shudder*: Martin, 4
young men: MacCallum Scott, *Clydesdale Man*, 39
sport: Steuart, 139

DANNY LONGLEGS

59   *pleasant kind of melancholy*: Steuart, 50
    small: Ibid., 13
    dark-haired: Ibid., illustration, 28
    family names: Ibid., 16

60   *accident*: Ibid., 20
    "gley'd een": Ibid., 34
    dumb-bells: Ibid., 50
    digitalis: Ibid., 51
    cousin: Ibid., 47
    gangrel: Ibid., 51

61   *short walks*: Ibid.
    Botany: Ibid., 50
    The "Green": Ibid., 23
    in spate: Ibid., 25

62   *braes*: Ibid., 50

DRAWING TEETH

63   *violent antipathy*: MacCallum Scott, *Clydesdale Man*, 38
    sixpence: Rankin, 'Notes', University of Glasgow Archives & Special
    Collections. GB 247 MS Murray 153–155, Appended Letter, 3
    rope: MacCallum Scott, *Clydesdale Man*, 38

64   *chair*: MacCallum Scott, 'Writings', 62
    George Brown: MacCallum Scott, *Clydesdale Man*, 38

DARWIN'S BULLDOG

66   *caused uproar*: Martin, 6
    ape: Gordon, 'How oddly', 12
    mind quite brilliant: Ibid., 11
    correspondence: Steuart, 125

67   *Letter from T.H. Huxley*: Ibid., 126

SANNIE BASIL

68   *real name*: MacCallum Scott, *Clydesdale Man*, 30
    laziness: Ibid., 31
    "souples": Ibid.

69   *oatmeal*: Ibid.
    divot house: Ibid.

HUNTER OF "THE DALES"

70   *rivalry*: MacCallum Scott, *Clydesdale Man*, 41
    spring of 1868: The Carluke and Lanark Gazette, 5 October 1912, 4c
    "Wild West": Macnair and Mort, 229

71   'Hunter of "The Dales"': Ibid., 228
    Dr John Selkirk: Ibid., 230

72 *Selkirk's sister*: The Carluke and Lanark Gazette, 5 October 1912, 4c
  '*auld tings!*': MacCallum Scott, *Clydesdale Man*, 35
  Daleville: Macnair and Mort, 231
  brass plate: MacCallum Scott, *Clydesdale Man*, 42

STANDING ON MY HEAD

73 *Maggie*: MacCallum Scott, *Clydesdale Man*, 43
  wholesome breakfast: Steuart, 115
  yoga: Gray, 286
  underclothes: Steuart, 110
  shaving: Ibid., 112
  pills: Ibid., 111

74 *orphan*: Ibid., 111–112
  medical certificate: Anon. [Rankin], 118
  ' "*Legstrong*"': Macnair and Mort, 132

BLUNT BOB

75 *Middle Ward*: Chambers, 347
  "*Orchard*": MacCallum Scott, *Clydesdale Man*, 8

76 *Agnes Lindsay*: Ibid.
  son: Ibid., 12
  "*Boatie*" *Thomson*: Ibid.
  1831: Peter J. Gordon. 'Scott Family of Carluke and Crossford:
  Gowanglen and Orchard', 5 January 2007, genealogy.com/forum/
  surnames/scott/16083/
  "*gey blunt*": MacCallum Scott, *Clydesdale Man*, 79
  wife: Ibid., 75
  remarry: Ibid., 77
  turn grey: Ibid., 79
  fruit: Ibid., 33

77 *lepers*: Ibid., 37

A THING OF BEAUTY

78 *skulls*: MacCallum Scott, *Clydesdale Man*, 38
  sleep and infantile form: Anon. [Rankin], 318–319

79 *twa farmers*: MacCallum Scott, *Clydesdale Man*, 40
  empty: Statham, 393(c)
  "*the Warlock*": Anon. [Rankin], 192

80 *Letter to John Young*: D[aniel] R[eid] Rankin, ALS to John Young,
  under-keeper of the Hunterian Museum. In John Greenshields,
  'Photographs of models of "The Jolly Beggars"', circa 1875, (Accession
  No. 242782) BNS 15 PHO, Robert Burns Collection, Special
  Collections, The Mitchell Library, Glasgow

MAGGIE

81   *Maggie died*: NRS. Statutory Registers Deaths 629/ Carluke 83
      Bob Pettigrew: MacCallum Scott, *Clydesdale Man*, 43
      black cloth: NRS. Glasgow Sheriff Court Wills, SC36/51/84, 587
      surprised: MacCallum Scott, *Clydesdale Man*, 43
      No gingerbread: NRS. Glasgow Sheriff Court Wills, SC36/51/84, 587

      A WIDOW FRIENDSHIP

82   *note*: Steuart, 138
      widow: Ibid., 139
      Letter to Marion: Walter O. Steuart. 'Books & Other Documents
      relating to Dr D.R. Rankin', Other Documents No. 9, Edinburgh: April
      1955. Courtesy of Carluke Parish Historical Society
      friendship: Steuart, 139

83   *somewhere*: Tennyson, 7

      DANNY RETURNS

84   *My legs*: Letter from Daniel Rankin Steuart to his brother John, dated
      31st August, 1879. Steuart, 146
      6 feet 8 inches: Peter J. Gordon. E-mail to a friend, 15 January 2009
      Chief Chemist: Steuart, 73
      serious designs: Ibid., 74

85   *paralysed*: Ibid., 116
      winter: Ibid., 131
      'praying for you': Ibid., 116
      sharp: Ibid., 146
      hair: The Carluke and Lanark Gazette, 5 March 1926, 2f
      geological specimens: Anon. *Proceedings of the Natural History Society
      of Glasgow*, 222
      'D.R. Rankin, Carluke Oct 31, 1880': Pen Portrait of Dr Rankin by
      Daniel Rankin Steuart. 'Books & Other Documents relating to Dr D.R.
      Rankin', Photographs No. 2, Edinburgh: April 1955

      DINNER WITH THE DEIL

86   *A terrific gale*: The Glasgow Herald, 23 November 1881, 5a
      Rev. Hobart!: Steuart, 116
      blown in: The Glasgow Herald, 23 November 1881, 5f

87   *nodded my assent*: Steuart, 116

      MORNING SUNRISE

88   *brightness*: Steuart, 116
      funeral: NRS. Glasgow Sheriff Court Wills, SC36/51/84, 587
      place of rest: Ibid.

      THE HAMILTON ADVERTISER 25 MARCH, 1882

89   *'Death of Dr Rankin'*: The Hamilton Advertiser, 25 March 1882, 1e
      morning of the 21st: NRS. Statutory Registers Deaths 629/ Carluke 36

BIBLIOGRAPHY

ADDISON, William Innes. *A Roll of the Graduates of the University of Glasgow from 31st December, 1727 to 31st December, 1897.* Glasgow: James MacLehose & Sons, 1898.

————. *The Matriculation Albums of the University of Glasgow from 1728 to 1858.* Glasgow: James MacLehose & Sons, 1913.

AGASSIZ, Louis. *Recherches sur les Poissons Fossiles.* (Five volumes) Tome I, Chapter I. Neuchâtel, Switzerland: Imprimerie de Petitpierre, 1833-1843.

ANON. *Prize-Essays and Transactions of the Highland and Agricultural Society of Scotland.* Vol. XIV. Edinburgh: William Blackwood and Sons, 1843.

ANON. *Proceedings of the Royal Physical Society of Edinburgh (1854-1858).* Vol. I. Edinburgh: Printed for the Society by Neill and Company, 1858.

ANON. [Daniel Reid Rankin]. *Notices Historical, Statistical & Biographical, Relating to The Parish of Carluke, from 1288 till 1874.* Glasgow: William Rankin, 1874.

ANON. ["Nestor"]. *Rambling Recollections of Old Glasgow.* Glasgow: John Tweed, 1880.

ANON. *Proceedings of the Natural History Society of Glasgow.* Vol. V, 1880-1883. Glasgow: Published by the Society at its Rooms, 207 Bath Street, 1884.

BURNETT, John. *Robert Burns and the Hellish Legion.* Edinburgh: 2009. Courtesy of National Museums of Scotland Enterprises Limited (publisher).

CHAMBERS, Robert. *The Picture of Scotland.* Vol. First, 2nd Ed. Edinburgh: William Tait, 1828.

COUTTS, James. *A History of the University of Glasgow.* Glasgow: James MacLehose and Sons, 1909.

DUNCAN, Alexander. *Memorials of the Faculty of Physicians and Surgeons of Glasgow 1599-1850.* Glasgow: James MacLehose and Sons, 1896.

GORDON, John (editor). *The New Statistical Account of Scotland.* Vol. VI. Edinburgh: William Blackwood and Sons, 1845.

GORDON, Peter J. 'How oddly all this touches me', 12 Feb 2009. holeousia.com/2013/03/17/how-oddly-all-this-touches-me. Courtesy of Dr Peter J. Gordon.

GRAY, Margaret Kingsley. 'A Doctor of Distinction'. *The Scots Magazine.* Dundee: December 1986. Courtesy of DC Thomson (publisher).

LACEPÈDE, Monsieur le Comte de. *Histoire naturelle des quadrupèdes-ovipares.* Tome Premier. Paris: Rapet, 1819.

MACCALLUM SCOTT, Alexander. *John Scott: A Clydesdale Man.* Dorset: Unpublished manuscript, June 1916. Courtesy of Dr Peter J. Gordon.

———. 'Writings of Alexander MacCallum Scott'. fl. 1893-1928. Courtesy of University of Glasgow Archives & Special Collections.

MACKENZIE, Peter. *Reminiscences of Glasgow and the West of Scotland.* Vol. II. Glasgow: John Tweed, 1866.

MACLACHLAN and Stewart (publisher). *The Medical Calendar: Or Student's Guide to the Medical Schools.* Edinburgh: Maclachlan & Stewart, 1828.

MACNAIR, Peter and Frederick Mort (editors). *History of the Geological Society of Glasgow, 1858-1908.* Glasgow: Published by the Society at its Rooms, 207 Bath Street, 1908.

MARTIN, Daniel. 'Dr Daniel Reid Rankin 1805-1882: A Life Sketch'. Carluke: Unpublished manuscript. Courtesy of Carluke Parish Historical Society.

McFEAT, W. and Co. (publisher). *The Glasgow Directory: Containing a List of the Merchants, Manufacturers, Traders, in the City and Suburbs.* Glasgow: W. McFeat, Stationer and Librarian, 1826.

MURRAY, David. *Memories of the Old College of Glasgow.* Glasgow: Jackson, Wylie and Co, 1927.

RAMSAY, Edward Bannerman. *Reminiscences of Scottish Life and Character.* Edinburgh: Edmonston and Douglas, 1867.

RANKIN, Daniel Reid. 'Notes for a history of Carluke'. 1870-1878. Courtesy of University of Glasgow Archives & Special Collections.

SKIPPEN, Mark et al. 'The Chain Saw—A Scottish Invention'. *Scottish Medical Journal.* Vol. 49 (2): 4. London: Sage Publications, 1 May 2004.

STATHAM, Henry Heathcote (editor). 'The Builder', Vol. LXI, No. 2546. London: 21 November 1891.

STEUART, Daniel Rankin. *Bygone Days: Some Recollections and Other Family Stories.* Edinburgh: Dunedin Press Ltd., 1936.

TENNYSON, Alfred. *Harold: A Drama.* London: Henry S. King & Co., 1877.

URIE, John. *Glasgow and Paisley Eighty Years Ago.* Paisley: Alexander Gardner, 1910.

YOUNG, John. *On the Carboniferous Fossils of the West of Scotland.* Glasgow: Published by the Geological Society of Glasgow at its Rooms, 207 Bath Street, 1871.